DAYS OF **PRAYER & FASTING**

A fasting guide for spiritual breakthroughs

Gary Rohrmayer

21 Days of Prayer & Fasting
A Fasting Guide for Spiritual Breakthroughs
Written by Gary Rohrmayer

Converge MidAmerica
924 Busse Hwy
Park Ridge, IL 60046

In fasting we do not bend God toward us,
but through fasting we bend our hearts
toward him."

Gary Rohrmayer

Foreword

A letter from Scott Ridout

"Then he said to his disciples, 'The harvest is plentiful but the workers are few. Ask the Lord of the harvest, therefore, to send out workers into his harvest field,'" (Matthew 9:37-38).

Jesus has commissioned us to reach the world with the gospel of Jesus (Matthew 28:18-20). God has given us his Holy Spirit to empower us as witnesses (Acts 1:8). The Spirit continually works in our lives to convict us of sin (John 16:8), guide us into truth (John16:13) and comfort us in trials (John 14:16). The Spirit accomplished his work in us, so that God can do his work through us. Scripture reminds us that our power used by God to effect change in this world begins with prayer (James 5:16).

Ours is a spiritual endeavor. We are completely dependent on God to change hearts (Ezekiel 36:26), open doors (Colossians 4:3) and cause growth (1 Corinthians 3:6-7). Jesus reminds us that some things can only be accomplished through prayer (Matthew 17:22). He reminds us that communion with him is a catalyst for fruitful ministry and that apart from him we can do nothing (John 15:5).

I have sensed our need as a movement to return to a foundation of corporate prayerfulness. Converge exists to glorify God by starting and strengthening churches together worldwide — and our practices need to be undergirded with our prayerfulness.

We will accomplish nothing in our own wisdom or power — we are completely dependent on God. The key to our fruitfulness, according to Jesus, is knowing him, abiding in him, connecting with him, relying on him, seeking his will and doing all things in his power and for his glory. True fruitfulness will not happen without true faithfulness in prayer.

Will you join me for the next 21 days in praying for God's leading in our lives, our churches, our movement, our mission fields and our 10-year vision? Will you take time to fast, giving up physical sustenance to be filled spiritually by God in preparation for this next season? Will you pray expectantly that God will display his power and faithfulness to us in this season? I believe as we come together, fully submitted to God in prayer, he will display both his person and his power in unprecedented ways. And he will advance the gospel so that more people will meet, know and follow him.

Scott Ridout,
Converge president

Why
prayer and fasting?

When was the last time you entered an extended time of prayer and fasting for spiritual, relational or missional breakthrough? Throughout the history of God's people, great leaders reached out to God for a fresh encounter or divine intervention.

Moses, in seeking a spiritual breakthrough, spent 40 days alone with God without eating or drinking until he received The Ten Commandments (Exodus 24:38).

King David sought a personal breakthrough as he fasted to keep himself humble (Psalm 35:13).

Ezra was seeking a breakthrough as he called God's people to fast and pray for protection against their enemies (Ezra 8:21-23).

Daniel fasted and prayed as he sought a restorative breakthrough for the exiled people living in rebellion against their God (Daniel 9:3-4).

The apostle Paul fasted as he pondered his breakthrough encounter with the risen Lord Jesus and what it meant for his life (Acts 9:9).

The leaders of the church in Antioch worshiped, prayed and fasted together as they sought missional breakthrough for their thriving church (Acts 13:1-3).

Our Savior, setting the supreme example, entered 40 days of fasting before launching his public ministry (Matthew 4:1-2).

What breakthrough are you seeking?

God's people all over the world have been seeking spiritual breakthroughs through prayer and fasting since the birth of the church.

What is the great matter in front of you? A loved one far from Christ? A critical decision in the life of your family? A relationship that is falling apart?

What great matters are in front of your church or ministry? An evangelistic outreach? A financial crisis? A leadership transition? Missional expansion?

Take time to write down each needed breakthrough and lift them up to God in prayer.

What is fasting?

Fasting is deliberately abstaining from the normal routines of life. Its purpose is to spend focused time in prayer and the study of God's word, seeking to align our lives with God's will.

Ultimately, fasting is more about replacing than abstaining. It is filling our lives with God's word instead of with food, social media or entertainment. It is finding satisfaction and enjoyment in God and in God alone. Fasting helps us humble ourselves before the Lord and positions us to experience spiritual breakthroughs in our lives.

Mathew Henry writes, "Fasting is of use to put an edge upon prayer." Have your prayers lost their fervor? Has your devotional life become dull? Fasting has a way of mystically sharpening our souls and making us more sensitive to the prompting of the Holy Spirit.

As Alex Gee said, "Fasting is not about changing God. It is not a mystical exercise to gain God's approval. Fasting is not about changing my world, but about letting God realign my heart toward his purposes."

We recognize as we begin this 21-day fast and prayer commitment that as God's people we need to boldly ask him for breakthroughs in any heartbreak, challenge or opportunity facing us individually and corporately.

How to get started

1 Pick your fast

Full Fast: Drink liquids only. Please consult your doctor first.

Daniel Fast: Eat only vegetables, fruit, water and juice (minimal amount of carbohydrates).

Partial Fast: Not eating one or two meals on a specific day or abstaining from certain kinds of food.

All-day Food Fast: Abstaining from food one day or multiple days per week.

Activity/Media Fast: Forgoing a time-consuming activity such as entertainment, hobbies, television, internet, sports, etc.

2 Set goals & write them down

Begin with clear personal goals as well as breakthrough goals for your church. Be specific. Why are you fasting? Do you need direction, healing, restoration of your marriage or resolution of family issues? Are you facing difficulties? Pray and ask the Holy Spirit for guidance. Write these requests in a journal or a notebook, or create a digital journal using your favorite notetaking program or app. Keeping a journal throughout your fast is a great way to track and remember all God does during your fast.

3 Feast on the word of God

Fasting is ultimately an expression of humility and dependence on God. It is about replacing the daily intake of food, entertainment and human contact with focused times of prayer, spending large amounts of time feeding on the Word of God and spiritual listening. You can use the recommended readings in this guide or continue your normal Bible reading program. The YouVersion Bible App and bible.com have a variety of 21-day Bible reading programs.

4 Open your life before God

One of the great benefits of spiritual fasting is a heightened awareness of God's presence and power in our lives. It is not that God has moved but that we have. Fasting has a great way of moving us towards a deeper spiritual dependency and away from willful self-dependency. The greatest breakthrough will take place when you make time to examine your life and discover what areas most need breakthrough. We ask that you fast for spiritual breakthroughs for your church family and its mission endeavors as well as for yourself.

5 Expect God to move

Enter your fast by faith. The Word of God says, "And without faith it is impossible to please God, for anyone who comes to him must believe that he exists and that he rewards those who earnestly seek him" (Hebrews 11:6). Spiritual fasting is a supernatural endeavor that has shaped and transformed God's people for centuries. If you have doubt, ask God to meet you in your doubts and lead you in overcoming them, just as the apostles prayed, "Increase our faith!" (Luke 17:5).

OUR PRAYER FOR YOU

Our prayer for you during the next 21 days is that you will experience a deeper craving for the beauty of the Lord and for the wonder of his leading in your life, and that you will know the fullness of the Holy Spirit and the favor of the God of heaven.

Our prayer is that you will realize you are not alone on this journey. You are joining with your immediate and extended church family in seeking God for significant breakthroughs. These will ripple out and turn into a tidal wave of revival and spiritual awakening across our country.

Our prayer is that you will acquire your own prayer-and-fasting testimony. And that God will overwhelm you with his goodness as you seek his power, presence and provision in every step of your journey.

DAY 1

Assumed practice

Fasting is not an option but an assumed practice for the serious-minded follower of Jesus. Fasting is a spiritual discipline that believers throughout history incorporated into their daily lives. Jesus did not say, "If you fast," but, "When you fast."

Scripture reading
Matthew 6

Key passages
Matthew 6:16-18 — "When you fast, do not look somber as the hypocrites do, for they disfigure their faces to show men they are fasting. Truly I tell you, they have received their reward in full. But when you fast, put oil on your head and wash your face, so that it will not be obvious to others that you are fasting, but only to your Father, who is unseen; and your Father, who sees what is done in secret, will reward you."

Fasting thought
"Jesus takes it for granted that his disciples will observe the pious custom of fasting. Strict exercise of self-control is an essential feature of the Christian's life. Such customs have only one purpose — to make the disciples more ready and cheerful to accomplish those things which God would have done."
Dietrich Bonhoeffer

Prayer

Father in heaven, as I subdue the impulses of the flesh this day, I do so not to achieve anything, not to use fasting as a bargaining chip or as a manipulative ploy to get your attention. But I fast as an act of worship, to make myself ready and resolute to do your will with a cheerful heart. In Jesus' name I pray. Amen.

Prayer & fasting journal

DAY 2

Dependence

Fasting is a humbling experience that reveals who or what we really depend upon or are controlled by.

Scripture reading
Psalm 69

Key passages
Psalm 69:10 — "When I weep and fast..."

Fasting thought
"More than any other single discipline, fasting reveals the things that control us. This is a wonderful benefit to the true disciple who longs to be transformed into the image of Jesus Christ. We cover up what is inside us with food and other good things, but in fasting these things surface. If pride controls us, it will be revealed almost immediately — anger, bitterness, jealousy, strife, fear. If they are within us, they will surface during fasting. At first we will rationalize that our anger is due to our hunger. Then we know that we are angry because the spirit of anger is within us. We can rejoice in this knowledge because we know that healing is available through the power of Christ."

Richard Foster

Prayer

Father in heaven, as I move through this fast, I seek the transforming work of the gospel in my life. Reveal the controlling influences in my life. Grant me the courage to face them, to renounce them, to confess them and to surrender them into your healing hands. Draw me closer to you through this fast. In Jesus' precious name I pray. Amen.

Prayer & fasting journal

DAY 3

Spiritual inventory

Fasting is a holy and legitimate pursuit of a Holy God. It can be of great use in conducting a rigorous spiritual inventory of one's soul and spiritual fruitfulness.

Scripture reading
Psalm 35

Key passages
Psalm 35:13 — "I put on sackcloth and humbled myself with fasting. When my prayers returned to me unanswered...."

Fasting thought
"Let us say something about fasting, because many, for want of knowing its usefulness, undervalue its necessity, and some reject it as almost superfluous; while, on the other hand where the use of it is not well understood, it easily degenerates into superstition. Holy and legitimate fasting is directed to three ends; for we practice it either as a restraint on the flesh, to preserve it from licentiousness, or as a preparation for prayers and pious meditations, or as a testimony of our humiliation in the presence of God when we are desirous of confessing our guilt before him."

John Calvin

Prayer

Father in heaven, through your probing eyes search my heart and reveal to me the areas of my life that are hindering fellowship with you. Expose those areas of my life that are interfering with my spiritual fruitfulness. Grant me the courage to face them with faith and confess them fully and humbly before you. Father, I want more of you and to be fully used by you. Amen.

Prayer & fasting journal

DAY 4

Real hunger

Fasting is a struggle against the flesh and is emotionally and physically demanding; in this we discover what we really hunger for.

Scripture reading
Deuteronomy 8

Key passages
Deuteronomy 8:2-3 — "Remember how the LORD your God led you all the way in the desert these forty years, to humble you and to test you in order to know what was in your heart, whether or not you would keep his commands. He humbled you, causing you to hunger and then feeding you with manna, which neither you nor your ancestors had known, to teach you that man does not live on bread alone but on every word that comes from the mouth of the LORD."

Fasting thought
"Do you have a hunger for God? If we don't feel strong desires for the manifestation of the glory of God, it is not because we have drunk deeply and are satisfied. It is because we have nibbled so long at the table of the world. Our soul is stuffed with small things, and there is no room for the great. If we are full of what the world offers, then perhaps a fast might express, or even increase, our soul's appetite for God. Between the dangers of self-denial and self-indulgence is the path of pleasant pain called 'fasting.'"

John Piper

Prayer

Father in heaven, as I move forward in this fast, help me to turn every hunger pain, thought or craving towards you. Teach me to feed on your word and to find a deep satisfaction in your truth. Today, Father, I want to experience the sweetness of your word. Amen.

Prayer & fasting journal

DAY 5

Confession

Remember to accompany your fast with confession of sin. Confess your sin, your spiritual weaknesses, your lack of dependence on God; through this we can experience the cleansing forgiveness of Jesus Christ.

Scripture reading
I John 1-2

Key passages
I Samuel 7:6 — "When they had assembled at Mizpah, they drew water and poured it out before the LORD. On that day they fasted and there they confessed, 'We have sinned against the LORD.'"

Fasting thought
"Confession recognizes the absence of God's presence in our lives through our own willfulness or indifference. Fasting is an act of craving more of God's presence, power and purity in our lives and ministry. Confession is admitting there is something wrong between us and God. Fasting is longing for the fullness of God to flood our souls. When we practice confession in our fasting, our fasting becomes more than a tool to bring God back to us; it becomes an instrument moving us back to God because God never moves."

Gary Rohrmayer

Prayer

Father in heaven, show me through this fast those areas of spiritual weakness and self-reliance in my life so that I may confess them and receive your healing, cleansing and purifying forgiveness. Father, I want to experience a new level of spiritual refreshment and strength that can only come through you. In the strong name of Jesus Christ our Lord I pray. Amen.

Prayer & fasting journal

DAY 6

Yearnings

Fasting is ultimately a yearning for something missing. Something was previously experienced but now is absent from our lives.

Scripture reading
Matthew 9

Key passages
Matthew 9:14-15 — "Then John's disciples came and asked him, 'How is it that we and the Pharisees fast, but your disciples do not fast?' Jesus answered, 'How can the guests of the bridegroom mourn while he is with them? The time will come when the bridegroom will be taken from them; then they will fast.'"

Fasting thought
"Christian fasting, at its root, is the hunger or a homesickness for God. It tells only half the story of Christian fasting. Half of Christian fasting is that our physical appetite is lost because our homesickness for God is so intense. The other half is that our homesickness for God is threatened because our physical appetites are so intense. In the first half, appetite is lost. In the second half, appetite is resisted. In the first, we yield to the higher hunger that is. In the second, we fight for the higher hunger that isn't. Christian fasting is not only the spontaneous effect of a superior satisfaction in God; it is also a chosen weapon against every force in the world that would take that satisfaction away."

John Piper

Prayer

Father in heaven, fill my life with a deeper awareness of your presence and power in my life. Grant me a deeper hunger for you than for those creature comforts the world offers. Give me victory this day. In the strong name of Jesus Christ my Lord I pray. Amen.

Prayer & fasting journal

DAY 7

Discerning

Fasting is a tool that aids in discerning the call of God in our lives. Fasting helps us slow down and hear God's voice.

Scripture reading
Acts 9

Key passages
Acts 9:3-6, 9 — "As he neared Damascus on his journey, suddenly a light from heaven flashed around him. He fell to the ground and heard a voice say to him, 'Saul, Saul, why do you persecute me?' 'Who are you, Lord?' Saul asked. 'I am Jesus, whom you are persecuting,' he replied. 'Now get up and go into the city, and you will be told what you must do.'.... "So they led him by the hand into Damascus. For three days he was blind, and did not eat or drink anything."

Fasting thought
A discerning fast "involves focusing on our choices instead of on our foods and praying our decisions through to successful conclusions... this type of fast helps us receive God's wisdom to make our decisions. This type of fast is not for every minor decision in life, such as where to go for lunch or what minor purchase to make. A discerning fast offers help in weighty decisions such as choosing a mate, resigning from a job and other life-changing choices. Fasting brings more light into the application of good decision-making skills."
Elmer Towns

Prayer

Father in heaven, today in my fast I yield to you and seek your wisdom in my life. Through this fast today grant me a greater perspective on those decisions before me, both minor and major. I want your best in my life. Protect me from being impulsive and rash and guide me in your perfect ways. In Jesus' name I pray. Amen.

Prayer & fasting journal

Testimony

Bill Bright, the passionate leader of Campus Crusade for Christ International (CRU), had a powerful experience with God in the 1990s specifically around "fasting." Allow God to speak to you through his fasting testimony.

"I believe the power of fasting as it relates to prayer is the spiritual atomic bomb that our Lord has given us to destroy the strongholds of evil and usher in a great revival and spiritual harvest around the world. Increasingly, I have been gripped with a growing sense of urgency to call upon God to send revival to our beloved country. In the spring and summer of 1994, I had a growing conviction God wanted me to fast and pray for forty days for revival in America and for the fulfillment of the Great Commission in obedience to our Lord's command.

"At first I questioned, 'Is this truly God's call for me?' Forty days was a long time to go without solid food. But with each passing day, his call grew stronger and clearer. Finally, I was convinced. God was calling me to fast, and he would not make such a call without a specific reason or purpose. With this conviction, I entered my fast with excitement and expectancy mounting in my heart, praying, 'Lord, what do you want me to do?'

"I believe such a long fast was a sovereign call of God because of the magnitude of the sins of America and of the Church. The Lord impressed that upon my heart, as well as the urgent need to help accelerate the fulfillment of the Great Commission in this generation.

"As I began my fast, I was not sure I could continue for forty days. But my confidence was in the Lord to help me. Each day his presence encouraged me to continue. The longer I fasted, the more I sensed the presence of the Lord. The Holy Spirit refreshed my soul and spirit, and I experienced the joy of the Lord as seldom before. Biblical truths leaped at me from the pages of God's Word. My faith soared as I humbled myself and cried out to God and rejoiced in his presence.

"This proved to be the most important 40 days of my life. As I waited upon the Lord, the Holy Spirit gave me the assurance that America and much of the world will, before the end of the year 2000, experience a great spiritual awakening. This divine visit from heaven will kindle the greatest spiritual harvest in the history of the Church. But before God comes in revival power, the Holy Spirit will call millions of God's people to repent, fast, and pray in the spirit of 2 Chronicles 7:14: 'If my people, who are called by my name, will humble themselves and pray and seek my face and turn from their wicked ways, then I will hear from heaven and will forgive their sin and will heal their land.'

"The scope of this revival depends on how believers in America and the rest of the world respond to this call. I have spent 50 years studying God's Word and listening to his voice, and his message could not have been clearer."

 I believe the power of fasting as it relates to prayer is the spiritual atomic bomb that our Lord has given us to destroy the strongholds of evil and usher in a great revival and spiritual harvest around the world."

Bill Bright

(Source: www.cru.org)
(Photo courtesy of Guy Gerrard/Worldwide Challenge)

DAY 8

Replacing vs. Abstaining

Fasting is more about replacing than it is about abstaining — replacing normal daily activities with focused praying, confessing, feeding on the Word and worshiping the Lord.

Scripture reading
Nehemiah 9

Key passages
Nehemiah 9:1-3 — "On the twenty-fourth day of the same month, the Israelites gathered together, fasting and wearing sackcloth and having dust on their heads....They stood at their places and read from the Book of the Law of the LORD their God for a quarter of the day, and spent another quarter in confession and in worshiping the LORD their God."

Fasting thought
"We tend to think of fasting as going without food. But we can fast from anything. If we love music and decide to miss a concert in order to spend time with God, that is fasting. It is helpful to think of the parallel of human friendship. When friends need to be together, they will cancel all other activities in order to make that possible. There's nothing magical about fasting. It's just one way of telling God that your priority at that moment is to be alone with him, sorting out whatever is necessary, and you have cancelled the meal, party, concert or whatever else you had planned to do in order to fulfill that priority."

J. I. Packer

Prayer

Father in heaven, as I fast today, I desire to seek your face through earnest prayer and honest confession, feeding on large portions of your word and offering responsive praise. In Jesus' name I pray. Amen.

Prayer & fasting journal

DAY 9

Thirsts

Let your thirsts drive you to God that he may satisfy your desires and meet the needs of your soul.

Scripture reading
Psalm 63

Key passages
Psalm 63:1 — "You, God, are my God, earnestly I seek you; I thirst for you, my whole being longs for you, in a dry and parched land where there is no water."

Fasting thought
"Prayer needs fasting for its full growth. Prayer is the one hand with which we grasp the invisible. Fasting is the other hand, the one with which we let go of the visible....Prayer is reaching out after the unseen; fasting is letting go of all that is seen and temporal. Fasting helps express, deepen, confirm the resolution that we are ready to sacrifice anything, even ourselves, to attain what we seek for the kingdom of God."

Andrew Murray

Prayer

Father in heaven, I reach out to you, the only one who can satisfy my thirsty heart and meet the needs within my soul. Through this fast may I crave you and your kingdom more and more. In Jesus' name I pray. Amen.

Prayer & fasting journal

DAY 10

Cravings

Fasting has a way of revealing what our hearts really crave. It can reveal what our soul needs and how we satisfy those deepest wants.

Scripture reading
Matthew 4

Key passages
Matthew 4:2-4 — "After fasting forty days and forty nights, he was hungry. The tempter came to him and said, 'If you are the Son of God, tell these stones to become bread.' Jesus answered, 'It is written: "Man does not live on bread alone, but on every word that comes from the mouth of God."'"

Fasting thought
"Fasting can be an expression of finding your greatest pleasure and enjoyment in life from God. That's the case when disciplining yourself to fast means you love God more than food, that seeking him is more important to you than eating. This honors God and is a means of worshiping him as God."

Donald Whitney

Prayer

Father in heaven, only you meet my deepest needs. Today grant me the ability to turn my hunger pains into moments of worship and praise, focusing on the beauty and splendor of your holiness and reveling in your infinite mercy. May you receive all the honor and praise as I come to you in the name of Jesus Christ our Lord. Amen.

Prayer & fasting journal

DAY 11

Cheerfulness

In fasting it is virtuous to conceal our suffering and discomfort with cheerfulness.

Scripture reading
Matthew 6

Key passages
Matthew 6:16-18 — "When you fast, do not look somber as the hypocrites do, for they disfigure their faces to show others they are fasting. Truly I tell you, they have received their reward in full. But when you fast, put oil on your head and wash your face, so that it will not be obvious to others that you are fasting, but only to your Father, who is unseen; and your Father, who sees what is done in secret, will reward you."

Fasting thought
"Let us learn from our Lord's instruction about fasting, the great importance of cheerfulness in our religion. Those words 'anoint thy head and wash thy face' are full of deep meaning. They should teach us to aim at letting men see we find that Christianity makes us happy. Never let us forget that there is not religion in looking melancholy and gloomy. Are we dissatisfied with Christ's wages and Christ's service? Surely not! Then let us not look as if we were."

J. C. Ryle

Prayer

Father in heaven, let me finish this fast with joy and cheerfulness as I feed on your beauty, truth and goodness. May every growl of my stomach, every internal complaint and headache be turned into moments of dependence on you and delight in every spiritual blessing I have in Christ. In the precious name of Jesus I pray. Amen.

Prayer & fasting journal

DAY 12

Satisfaction

Fasting is rewarded because it is a cry from the heart of those who find their ultimate satisfaction in God and in God alone.

Scripture reading
Psalm 73

Key passages
Psalm 73:25-26 —"Whom have I in heaven but you? And earth has nothing I desire besides you. My heart and my flesh may fail, but God is the strength of my heart and my portion forever."

Fasting thought
"When God sees the confession of need and this expression of trust, he acts, because the glory of his all-sufficient grace is at stake. The final answer is that God rewards fasting because fasting expresses the cry of the heart that nothing on earth can satisfy our souls besides God. God must reward this cry because God is most glorified in us when we are most satisfied in him."

John Piper

Prayer

Father, whom have I in heaven but you? And besides you I desire nothing on earth. My heart and my flesh may fail. But you are the strength of my heart and my portion forever and ever. I declare this in the precious name of Jesus. Amen.

Prayer & fasting journal

DAY 13

Sacrifice

Are you tired of fasting? Fasting is a sacrificial act that realigns our affections, moving them from the temporal to the eternal. It turns each moment of craving into a prayer of intense dependence.

Scripture reading
Psalm 109

Key passages
Psalm 109:24 — "My knees give way from fasting; my body is thin and gaunt."

Fasting thought
"If religion requires us to sometimes fast and deny our natural appetites, it is to lessen that struggle and war that is in our nature; it is to render our bodies fitter instruments of purity, and more obedient to the good motions of divine grace; it is to dry up the springs of our passions that war against the soul, to cool the flame of our blood, and render the mind more capable of divine meditations. So that although these abstinences give some pain to the body, yet they so lessen the power of bodily appetites and passions, and so increase our taste of spiritual joys, that even these severities of religion, when practiced with discretion, add much to the comfortable enjoyment of our lives."

William Law

Prayer

Father in heaven, my flesh is tired, my spirit is weakening; grant me the mental focus, spiritual awareness and physical will to push through the quitting points as I seek to realign my desires to your perfect will and your mission and for your glory. In Jesus' name I pray. Amen.

Prayer & fasting journal

DAY 14

Authentic fasting

Fasting must be accompanied with goodwill and good works toward others to be effective and pleasing to God.

Scripture reading
Isaiah 58

Key passages
Isaiah 58:3-4 — "'Why have we fasted,' they say, 'and you have not seen it? Why have we humbled ourselves, and you have not noticed?' "Yet on the day of your fasting, you do as you please and exploit all your workers. Your fasting ends in quarreling and strife, and in striking each other with wicked fists. You cannot fast as you do today and expect your voice to be heard on high."

Fasting thought
"Why is this fasting unacceptable to God? What's wrong with it? What's wrong with it is that it left the sin in their lives untouched. The only authentic fasting is fasting that includes a spiritual attack against our own sin. Whatever else we fast for, we must fast for our own holiness. We cannot fast for anything with authenticity while living in known sin."

John Piper

Prayer

Father in heaven, grant me the faith to move closer to the light of God's holiness and to deal with the darkness of my own soul. Grant me the courage through this fast to examine my attitudes and behaviors toward those around me and to make right any wrongs for which I am responsible. Father, I desire that my fast be acceptable to you. In Jesus' name I pray. Amen.

Prayer & fasting journal

Testimony

David Brainerd, a young missionary in his 20s, understood the need for fasting in the advancement of the gospel as well as in the expansion of his soul. Here is a brief testimony from his diary:

"Feeling somewhat the sweetness of communion with God and the force of his love and how it captivates my soul and makes all my desires and affections to center in God, I set apart this day for fasting and prayer to God, to bless me in view of preaching the gospel. I had life and power in prayer this afternoon. God enabled me to wrestle ardently in intercession for my friends. The Lord visited me marvelously in prayer. I think my soul was never in such agony before. I felt no restraint, for the treasures of God's grace were opened to me. I wrestled for absent friends and for the ingathering of poor souls. I was in such agony from sun half an hour high till near dark that I was all over wet with sweat. Oh! My dear Savior did sweat blood for these poor souls! I longed for more compassion toward them. I was under a sense of divine love and went to bed in such a frame of mind, with my heart set on God."

(Source: Journey With David Brainerd, by Richard A. Hasler)

> The Lord visited me marvelously in prayer. I think my soul was never in such agony before. I felt no restraint, for the treasures of God's grace were opened to me."

David Brainerd
Missionary

DAY 15

Fasting and God's freedom

Fasting is a means of seeing spiritual breakthrough for a physical or emotional problem as well as finding freedom from the besetting sins that affect our relationship with God. Today focus your prayers on those hurts, habits and hangups you need spiritual healing to overcome.

Scripture reading
Isaiah 58

Key passages
Isaiah 58:6 — "Is not this the kind of fasting I have chosen: to loosen the chains of injustice and untie the cords of the yoke, to set the oppressed free and break every yoke?"

Fasting thought
"The Elijah Fast is not a common corrective device to be used for freeing yourself from minor habits. It is called for in severely negative cases of mental and emotional response. It often works because it is a discipline that builds self-discipline and self-esteem. But more important than psychological esteem, the Elijah Fast invites God into the problem. Then, in the strength of God, victory is possible."
Elmer Towns

Prayer

Father in heaven, you are the great physician, you are the healer of my soul, you are one who grants victory over my emotional wounds that are the cause of my destructive thinking and debilitating habits. During my fast bring to light those besetting sins that hurt my relationship with you and my effectiveness in your mission. May I experience a new level of freedom and victory as I lean into you this day during my fast. In Jesus' name I pray. Amen.

Prayer & fasting journal

DAY 16

Fasting and God's refreshment

Our fasting may be rewarded in the experience not only of spiritual replenishment but also of physical refreshment.

Scripture reading
Isaiah 58

Key passages
Isaiah 58:6,8,11 — "Is not this the kind of fasting I have chosen: ...and your healing will quickly appear...and will strengthen your frame."

Fasting thought
"Of fasting I say this: It is right to fast frequently in order to subdue and control the body. For when the stomach is full, the body does not serve for preaching, for praying, for studying or for doing anything else that is good. Under such circumstances God's Word cannot remain. But one should not fast with a view to meriting something by it as by a good work."

Martin Luther

Prayer

Father in heaven, as I subdue my flesh and control my appetite today, refresh my spirit, replenish my soul, heal my wounds and strengthen my will to carry out your desires. I ask this in the strong name of Jesus Christ my Lord. Amen.

Prayer & fasting journal

DAY 17

Fasting and God's light

Approached properly, fasting can bring light into our darkness and clarity to our confusion.

Scripture reading
Isaiah 58 & Psalm 112

Key passages
Isaiah 58:8,10 — "Then your light will break forth like the dawn...then your light will rise in the darkness, and your night will become like the noonday."

Fasting thought
"By aligning our hearts with God through fasting, we find ourselves consumed by his resplendent nature. This is like the sun breaking forth through the early morning darkness. This breakthrough comes as he turns the gloom and confusion of our darkness into his light of love, joy and peace."

Gary Rohrmayer

Prayer

Father of Light, as I fast today, blast through the darkness I am facing with the light of your love. Transform the gloom of discouragement with the hope of your pure light. Help me see through the falsehood of darkness and behold the blazing truth of your light. In Jesus' name I pray. Amen.

Prayer & fasting journal

DAY 18

Fasting and God's victory

Fasting is a weapon used to respond to the present and future attacks of the evil one.

Scripture reading
Esther 4

Key passages
Isaiah 58:6, 8 — "Is not this the kind of fasting I have chosen...then your righteousness will go before you, and the glory of the LORD will be your rear guard."

Esther 4:15 — "Go, gather together all the Jews who are in Susa, and fast for me. Do not eat or drink for three days, night or day. I and my attendants will fast as you do. When this is done, I will go to the king, even though it is against the law. And if I perish, I perish."

Fasting thought
"When the devil, the foe and the tyrant, sees a man bearing this weapon [fasting], he is straightway frightened and he recollects and considers that defeat which he suffered in the wilderness at the hands of the Savior; at once his strength is shattered and the very sight of this weapon, given us by our Commander-in-Chief, burns him."
Isaac of Syria

Prayer

Father in heaven, Lord Almighty, today through my fast I seek to be better prepared for the spiritual battles that I am engaged in. I choose to stand firm in you. I choose to live my life by the truth of God and not by the lies of the enemy. I choose to live righteously and not selfishly. I choose to live by faith and not by sight, extinguishing every attack from the enemy. I choose to live by the power of the Word of God. In the strong name of Jesus my Lord I pray. Amen.

Prayer & fasting journal

DAY 19

Fasting and the presence of God

Are you being surprised in your fasting experience? God loves to surprise his children by strangely satisfying them with his presence.

Scripture reading
Isaiah 58 & Psalm 1

Key passages
Isaiah 58:6,11 — "Is not this the kind of fasting I have chosen….he will satisfy your needs in a sun-scorched land and will strengthen your frame. You will be like a well-watered garden, like a spring whose waters never fail."

Fasting thought
"The rewards of fasting are not often instantaneous but are experienced over time. They come as surprises, like in the midst of a worship service when my soul is stirred and strangely satisfied. Or when I am reading the Word and my inner being is lifted beyond this world with a fresh perspective. Or when I am in prayer and the groaning of my heart experiences a peace that is unexplainable. I have found the rewards ultimately lead to a more intimate and satisfying experience with the God who made me, saves me and fills me."

Gary Rohrmayer

Prayer

Father in heaven, today during my fast may I experience the sweet satisfying nature of your presence and experience the refreshing power of your abiding strength. Father, for your honor and glory I want to be like a well-watered garden, like a spring that never runs dry. In Jesus' name I pray. Amen.

Prayer & fasting journal

DAY 20
Fasting and God's guiding hand

Fasting has its spiritual rewards. One of the rewards of fasting is experiencing the guiding hand of God in our lives.

Scripture reading
Isaiah 58; Psalm 23

Key passages
Isaiah 58: 6,11 — "Is not this the kind of fasting I have chosen...And the LORD will guide you always; he will satisfy your needs in a sun-scorched land and will strengthen your frame."

Fasting thought
"Every time I have fasted, I have found my worship experience sweeter. I found the illumination of God's Spirit brighter and my hunger for God's word stronger. Through my fasting God has guided me, comforted me, challenged me and corrected me. It is not that I have bent God toward me through fasting, but that I, through fasting, have bent my heart toward him."

Gary Rohrmayer

Prayer

Father in heaven, I want to experience your guiding and empowering hand on my life and ministry. There is nothing like knowing that the hand of the Lord is on my life. Today through my fasting I bend my heart and my will toward you and your ways. In Jesus' name I pray. Amen.

Prayer & fasting journal

DAY 21

A holy habit

Fasting is a discipline that should be a holy habit.

Scripture reading
Matthew 9

Key passages
Matthew 9:14-15 —"Then John's disciples came and asked him, 'How is it that we and the Pharisees fast often, but your disciples do not fast?' "Jesus answered, 'How can the guests of the bridegroom mourn while he is with them? The time will come when the bridegroom will be taken from them; then they will fast.'"

Fasting thought
"For the serious-minded follower of Jesus, fasting is a consistent habit. In a world filled with indulgences, we need, on a routine basis, to consciously lay aside our freedoms in Christ for the purpose of seeking the face of God, intimacy with the Son of God and fullness of the Holy Spirit."

Gary Rohrmayer

Prayer

Father in heaven, thank you for all you have done in my life over the past 21 days. My heart longs for you. My soul craves your presence. I need you. I worship you. I love you. Help me to make fasting a habit in my life. In the precious name of Jesus I pray. Amen.

Prayer & fasting journal

RESPOND

Has God given you a prayer & fasting testimony?

Experiencing the sweetness of his presence. Enjoying the wonders of his grace. Discovering his guiding hand in a major decision. Finding a new sense of freedom and healing from the hurts of the past. Realizing a victory over a nagging area of sin in your life. Embracing a spiritual breakthrough in your ministry.

How has God shown up in your life in the past 21 days of fasting? If he has, review your journal entries from the past 21 days or write about it now. Then share it with a friend and reflect upon it with a thankful heart. If he hasn't, keep fasting until he does. Be determined like Jacob, who wrestled with God and would not let him go until God blessed him. In this, Jacob experienced the transformational power of God that marked not only his life in that moment but also his descendants for eternity.

The great theologian Ole Hallesby wrote, "The purpose of fasting is to loosen to some degree the ties which bind us to the world of material things and our surroundings as a whole, in order that we may concentrate all our spiritual powers upon the unseen and eternal things."

May we all experience the blessedness of what Jesus taught his disciples, "Blessed are those who hunger and thirst for righteousness, for they will be filled." (Matthew 5:6)

Your testimony

EXTRA DAY

Fasting and the suffering world

Fasting is turning your hunger pain into requests, prayers and petitions for the suffering around you. Today focus your prayers on those suffering close to you and those suffering throughout the world.

Scripture reading
Isaiah 58; James 2:14-26

Key passages
Isaiah 58:6-7 — "Is not this the kind of fasting I have chosen....Is it not to share your food with the hungry and to provide the poor wanderer with shelter — when you see the naked, to clothe them, and not to turn away from your own flesh and blood?"

Fasting thought
"Fasting is a hard discipline to practice without it consuming all our attention. Yet when we use it as a part of prayer or service, we cannot allow it to do so. When a person chooses fasting as a spiritual discipline, he or she must, then, practice it well enough and often enough to become experienced in it, because only the person who is well habituated to systematic fasting as a discipline can use it effectively as a part of direct service to God, as in special times of prayer or other service."

Dallas Willard

Prayer

Father in heaven, today I turn my prayers towards all the suffering in our world. Make a way for food, clothing, shelter and medical supplies to reach those in critical need. Send medical help to those in need. Grant those who are serving the poor and needy your strength, wisdom, compassion and spiritual insight to care for them. In the merciful name of Jesus I pray. Amen.

Prayer & fasting journal

Thoughts

on prayer & fasting

"Christian fasting moves from broken and contrite poverty of spirit to sweet satisfaction in the free mercy of Christ and to ever greater desires and enjoyments of God's inexhaustible grace."
John Piper

"Fasting is an act of humility that spotlights our weaknesses and reveals dependence on things rather than on God."
Gary Rohrmayer

"Fasting tests where the heart is. And when it reveals that the heart is with God and not the world, a mighty blow is struck against Satan."
John Piper

"Fasting is more about longing for the power and presence of Jesus than restricting our appetites."
Gary Rohrmayer

"Fasting confirms our utter dependence upon God by finding in him a source of sustenance beyond food."
Dallas Willard

"Fasting helps to express, to deepen and to confirm the resolution that we are ready to sacrifice anything, even ourselves, to attain the Kingdom of God."
Andrew Murray

"Fasting is more about replacing than it is about abstaining — replacing normal activities with focused times of prayer and feeding on the Word of God."
Gary Rohrmayer

"Fasting is calculated to bring a note of urgency and importunity into our praying, and to give force to our pleading in the court of heaven. The man who prays with fasting is giving heaven notice that he is truly in earnest."
Arthur Wallis

"Fasting is not about changing God. It is not a mystical exercise to gain God's approval. Fasting is not about changing my world, but about letting God realign my heart toward his purposes."
Alex Gee

"Fasting is not a tool for gaining discipline or developing piety. Instead, fasting is the bulimic act of ridding ourselves of our fullness to attune our senses to the mysteries that swirl in and around us."
Dan B. Allender

"As soon as a Christian recognizes that he has failed in his service... that all his joy in God has vanished and that his capacity for prayer has quite gone, it is high time for him to launch an assault upon the flesh, and prepare for better service by fasting and prayer."
Dietrich Bonhoeffer

"Fasting cleanses the soul, raises the mind, subjects one's flesh to the spirit, renders the heart contrite and humble, scatters the clouds of concupiscence, quenches the fire of lust, and kindles the true light of chastity."
Augustine

"Faith needs a life of prayer in which to grow and keep strong... prayer needs fasting for its full and perfect development."
Andrew Murray

"Fasting with a pure heart and motives, I have discovered, brings personal revival and adds power to our prayers."
Bill Bright

Fasting teaches that me that I Need to fill my stomach w/ God

"The rewards of fasting ultimately lead to a more intimate and satisfying experience with the God who made me."
Gary Rohrmayer

"More than any other single discipline, fasting reveals the things that control us."
Richard Foster

"A fast is not a hunger strike. Fasting submits to God's commands. A hunger strike makes God submit to our demands."
Ed Cole

"There's nothing magical about fasting. It's just one way of telling God that your priority at that moment is to be alone with him."
J. I. Packer

"Every time I have fasted I have found my worship experience sweeter, the illumination of God's Spirit brighter and the hunger for God's Word stronger."
Gary Rohrmayer

"Fasting is an act of humility. Fasting gives opportunity for deeper humility as we recognize our sins, repent, receive God's forgiveness and experience his cleansing of our soul and spirit. Fasting also demonstrates our love for God and our full confidence in his faithfulness."
Bill Bright

"Fasting possesses great power. If practiced with the right intention, it makes one a friend of God. The demons are aware of that."
Tertullian

"I desired as many as could to join together in fasting and prayer, that God would restore the spirit of love and of a sound mind."
John Wesley

"The Bible does not teach that fasting is a kind of spiritual hunger strike that compels God to do our bidding. If we ask for something outside of God's will, fasting does not cause him to reconsider. Fasting does not change God's hearing so much as it changes our praying."
Donald Whitney

"Fasting turns each moment of craving into a prayer of intense dependence."
Gary Rohrmayer

"Fasting, if we conceive of it truly, must not...be confined to the question of food and drink; fasting should really be made to include abstinence from anything which is legitimate in and of itself for the sake of some special spiritual purpose. There are many bodily functions which are right and normal and perfectly legitimate, but which for special peculiar reasons in certain circumstances should be controlled. That is fasting."
Martyn Lloyd-Jones

"Fasting from any nourishment, activity, involvement or pursuit—for any season—sets the stage for God to appear. Fasting is not a tool to pry wisdom out of God's hands or to force needed insight about a decision."
Dan B. Allender

"Fasting is abstaining from anything that hinders prayer."
Andrew Bonar

"So that although these abstinences give some pain to the body, yet they so lessen the power of bodily appetites and passions, and so increase our taste of spiritual joys, that even these severities of religion, when practiced with discretion, add much to the comfortable enjoyment of our lives."
William Law

✝ CONVERGE

Converge is a movement of churches working to help people meet, know and follow Jesus. We do this by starting and strengthening churches together worldwide.

For over 165 years we've helped churches like yours bring life change to communities in the U.S. and around the world through church planting and discipleship multiplication, leadership training and coaching and global missions.

We are rooted in the gospel and the infallible, inerrant word of God and the need for every person to surrender to Jesus for salvation. Our goal is to give every person the opportunity to hear the gospel, say "yes" to Jesus, grow in faith, be equipped to serve and be sent out. We are committed to seeing vibrant churches in every community, state and country within our reach. We want every person to experience a life-changing, personal relationship with Jesus. Our churches come together around something greater than a compelling mission. What brings us together is Christ's completed work on the cross. Because of the cross, we have forgiveness from our past, power for our present and hope for our future. As a result, we converge around the cross to take what Christ has done for us and make it known to others.

Throughout our history we have seen generations of churches, leaders and missionaries join forces through God's power to accomplish the impossible. His command to go and make disciples resonates in our hearts and churches. It is evident in the ministries of our congregations and mission fields.

As we continue to move forward, we are asking God to help us:

Open the front door to see more churches started, disciples multiplied and missionaries sent out.

Close the back door to develop more healthy, growing churches and leaders.

Tear down the walls to expand our cultural diversity and address racial barriers to advance the gospel.

Build the house to increase collaboration and resources needed to start and strengthen more churches.

We believe this emphasis will result in more followers of Jesus—who are focused on the mission of Jesus.

For more information about Converge, visit converge.org

About the author: Gary Rohrmayer

Gary Rohrmayer was born is Waukesha, Wisconsin. Growing up in a family of entrepreneurs, after a dramatic conversion he turned his entrepreneurial energy into starting new churches throughout the Midwest. As pastor, author, speaker, coach, trainer and leader, he has a unique focus in mobilizing and mentoring leaders in the mission of Jesus. He specializes in equipping leaders in areas of spiritual formation, church planting and church health. Gary has been a force in church planting since 1987. During this time, he has been involved in over 151 new church plants and trained thousands of church planters across the country. He currently is serving as the president and executive minister of Converge MidAmerica, overseeing its business and ministry interests that support regional church planting and ongoing care of its partner churches. Gary's vision is to see "that no leader travels their ministry journey alone."

41443219R00040

Made in the USA
Middletown, DE
06 April 2019